A Bag of Sins

Tina Jackson

ISBN: 978-1-969880-90-2

To you reading this story, I pray that whatever the enemy is speaking over you is broken off and sent back to the pits of hell by the blood of Jesus. You are set free, and there is peace and joy in the Lord. Cast all your cares upon Him, in Jesus' mighty name.

Amen.

Dedication

In Loving Memory and Gratitude

To honor my mom and grandson—there isn't a day that goes by that I don't think of you both. I miss you like crazy. God called you home, but I hold tightly to the cherished memories we shared.

Mom, your prayers have been answered. God saved me, and I know you're smiling down on me. Thank you for all the gatherings, the quick talks, and the love you poured into my life.

To my "Fat Fat," my sweet grandson, Grandma will always carry you in her heart. I look back at your pictures and see your beautiful soul shining through. Rest easy, both of you—no more pain. Glory be to God! As the Bible says, "Absent from the body is to be present with the Lord." I love you both forever. ❤️

To My Sons

Dennis, Kavan, Teyon, and Montel, I thank God every day for blessing me with you. Near or far, I carry you all in my heart. No matter what, my love for you is endless and unconditional. It's been a joy and a journey to have you as my sons. God bless you always!

To My Grandbabies

To all my precious grandchildren, I love you with all my heart. Always remember that Grandma loves you deeply, no matter what. You are all my pride and joy, and I will forever be here in spirit to love and guide you.

Dedication to the Pastors in My Life

Pastor Linda Caldwell-Boykin

I joined Salvation Outreach Deliverance Center in 2017, where I gave my life to Christ. A year later, I was baptized. God placed me there to become spiritually grounded. Pastor always reminded me of what God wanted from me and encouraged me to build a personal relationship with Him.

At the time, I didn't fully understand—but now, it all makes sense. One of the scriptures I've held onto during this journey is Philippians 4:19, "But my God shall supply all your need according to his riches in glory by Christ Jesus." And truly, God has provided— through your leadership, your prayers, and your wisdom. I'm so grateful and thankful. Pastor, you've been such a blessing. May God continue to bless you and use you mightily.

Faith at the Table Ministry – Pastor Dr. Anita Naves

Glory be to God! I joined Faith at the Table Ministry in 2020, and it's been an amazing journey ever since. I've witnessed every prophecy come to pass. The prayers, the covering, and the teaching—every bit of it has brought me closer to God.

Pastor, I've always felt your love and dedication, and I thank you for allowing God to speak through you. There were many days when your words reminded me of Hebrews 13:5, "He will never leave you nor forsake you."

Thank you so much for all that you do. Continue to let God use you for His glory. May He continue to bless and keep you always.

Acknowledgment

I want to give honor to God, who is the head of my life. I also want to give a shout-out to my pastor, Dr. Anita Naves, for always encouraging and covering me. Additionally, I extend my gratitude to my oldest son, Dennis Jackson, who has been right there through this whole project with powerful words from the Lord. Holy Spirit, guide and lead me every step of the way. Thank you for getting me through.

Contents

About the Author

Hi, I'm a blessed woman of God. My story is a true journey that needs to be shared around the world to show how amazing God is. This is His story and His book; I'm just the vessel. He took a party girl living a double life for over four decades and transformed me. If He did it for me, He can do it for you.

Chapter 1: A Battle Within

It was always very quiet in my world. I saw a lot but never said anything. I was always in deep thought, wondering about the future. I planned my life in my head, fantasizing for so long. I've always wondered how it would turn out, not realizing it was getting darker and darker.

Hi, I'm Tina. If you're reading this, take this journey with me.

I was born five months premature, a tiny thing, the size of a little rat, or so I was told. I spent weeks in the hospital incubator before I was allowed to come home. My mom told me she would sit me down anywhere in the house while she was cleaning, and all I did was stare. I would sit very close to the TV. When I was five, she took me to the hospital to get checked out because she was worried. The doctor said kids do that sometimes, nothing to worry about. But she wasn't satisfied, so she took me back a few weeks later. This time, the doctors ran tests, and after a few hours, they told her she got me there just in time—I would have gone blind.

So now, I needed surgery—many surgeries. They discovered I was born with cataracts, and I had to undergo eight to ten surgeries, visit after visit. I remember my mom changing my patch early in the morning and putting drops in both eyes every day until I was about eight or nine years old. From the age of five, that was a lot.

When I finally returned to school on a regular basis, I had one elementary friend who was cool and always looked out for me. I was a quiet little girl with big glasses, as thin as a toothpick. I got picked on and teased a lot, and it hurt. But in my mind, I created another world, one that no one knew about. It was dark and private—that's where all my secrets were, where I hid how I felt about people, my life, and my future.

My desires and cravings were for any woman or girl who gave me attention—my best friend, teachers, and these twins who were so nice to me. The feelings were strong, though now I realize it was more infatuation. As I grew older, by age 12, the desire became more intense, staying in my mind until it could become reality. I was very much a tomboy, strong and athletic, better at sports than a lot of the guys. I always wanted her to attend my games, to have someone close to me.

Around the age of 13, someone close in the family began to touch me in ways that weren't right. It happened many times, over and over, but I never said anything. I kept it in my vault of inner thoughts, always. I figured no one would believe me, and I was afraid. We used to lie on top of each other so many times. Going into my teens, high school was so different from elementary school. The girls were more developed, and during gym class, we would undress. Now, let me say this: not everyone was attractive, as people seemed to think. No. But there were a few I thought were beautiful, though I kept it to myself, staying very quiet. Still, I got picked on so much. The urges got stronger, out of control, so in my mind, it became reality. I could be whoever I wanted in my inner thoughts. I knew my mom and family would never understand. Faking an interest in boys was so painful. I just stared at them and laughed, always competing against them. I was the little girl with big glasses and a ponytail. They used to say, "She doesn't have a butt," and laugh. I felt so much sadness. I would retreat into my inner world and imagine if I did, if I had the perfect shape and was pretty. Who was I going to tell? I kept it all in my inner world.

At that point, I really lost interest in school. Every day I went only because my mom made me. It was a dark place. I struggled with classes and had to do summer school every year. By 9th grade, I just didn't care anymore. I started hanging out with a troubled girl who made me feel like I had some power. Everyone liked her, so I started cutting classes and getting into fights. We even went back to our elementary school just to mess around with the smaller kids. We messed around and got arrested. My mom was pregnant with my baby brother, and I was running wild at this point, running away from home. I felt like I was just trying to find my way, hanging with the worst people, starting to smoke and drink a little, coming home high. Nothing mattered anymore. School was a joke. So, every morning I got up like I was going to school, but instead, I just got high and roamed the streets. I really didn't know what I was doing, just thinking to myself how my grown life would be. I never understood why I was here.

Then one day, something happened that disappointed me. I didn't like rejection or disappointment; it hurt too much. When I think back over my life, writing this about myself, I thank God for the gift of love. I couldn't understand why everyone didn't love the same, so in my inner world, everyone did. What I realize now is that the emotions we feel every day have to be controlled, or they'll take us on an emotional rollercoaster. You can pretend so much that you start to believe it yourself. I self-medicated from the time I knew how, though I didn't know what I was doing. You just wonder, and I realize that the people you love, you just want to protect them. But sometimes, your protection can become obsession without you knowing it until they're gone or later. I've talked to several therapists over the years. Some understood me, sometimes. I used to just want someone to get it. In my life, I was called names and abandoned by people. All that time, God was there.

Your mind races so much. I thought I couldn't or wouldn't walk away from my family, but somehow, I did. When I finally found peace, I became fiercely protective of it—having never known protection myself. Someone out there right now is struggling within themselves and with their identity. The world will make you believe you have to go with the crowd just to feel love. I don't know you, but if you're reading this, I love you with the love of God. My life was like a ball of yarn, all wrapped up together, rolling here, there, everywhere. I didn't like the way I looked at all. I sat by myself. Oh, I get lonely at times, but I used to just invite anyone over to keep from being alone. No more sleeping with the enemy. Now, since I had an injury that changed my life, at one point depression tried to come in. When you're used to being independent, you don't know how to deal with it, but I kept trying. My profession as a chef gives me so much joy. Seeing people experience my food brings me happiness. I take all my hurt and pain to God, and He soothes me in my healing. I can't and will not change who I am. When I began writing about myself, I couldn't believe it. I'm so private and secretive, but God said to share my story, no matter how short or long. Somebody needs it to be transformed—from party girl, attractive to same-sex, drinking every day, fornicating, living recklessly, self-destructing—to living day to day, not caring, to being saved by the Lord, Savior Jesus Christ, and the Holy Spirit. He saved me and kept me with my bag of sins.

There's no way I'm supposed to keep this to myself. Do I still have battles? Of course, we all do. But I choose the Lord to fight all of them for me. Do I get tempted? Of course, but I go in prayer. Do I still have the desire for sex? Yes. He's got me in self-control. I have some days when prayer is deep because I'm still in the flesh. No matter what, now my job is to go around the world and tell others that Jesus Christ died for our sins. He can save you from anything. Take my story and learn that life is uplifting. Sharing my story has blessed me, and I hope it blesses you.

Even before I got saved, the Father above still covered and kept me, even when I was in a same-sex relationship. I couldn't go all the way with those women. There was always this weight

I felt, and I couldn't understand it myself. I found them attractive but couldn't give my all.

Chapter 2: The Walls Began To Fall

In my world it was always peace, everyone was against me. One day, I hopped on a metro bus and met this handsome guy. We began talking and exchanging numbers. We talked over and over on the phone; my family was moving soon, and the new place turned out to be closer to him. We started dating and were always together; we were inseparable and fell in love. After four years of our relationship, I discovered I was pregnant with my first son. Due to the age gap, my family always had a problem with our relationship. They started to question my baby, so I had to do a blood test; we were so in love, yet confused.

When I told him I was pregnant, he insisted on a paternity test. I didn't argue—he was the only man I'd been with. The test confirmed what I already knew, but instead of feeling relieved, I felt even more isolated. I tried to focus on my pregnancy, but I was overwhelmed with conflicting emotions. My mother reassured me that we would get through this together, but I still felt lost and uncertain. The first trimester was a blur of exhaustion and depression. I spent most of my time sleeping and eating, trapped in a cycle of despair. My thoughts constantly oscillated between hope and despair as I struggled to imagine a future where he might come back to me, we broke up shortly after that.

As my pregnancy progressed, I felt increasingly weighed down by my circumstances. The physical changes, the weight gain, and the emotional turmoil all took a toll on me. But somehow, I made it through. Nine months later, I gave birth to a healthy baby boy, weighing 7 pounds. Holding him in my arms, I felt a flicker of hope—a sense that maybe this could be a new beginning.

But reality quickly set in. He came to see the baby, bringing diapers and milk, but that was the extent of his involvement. It was a fleeting visit, and soon he was gone again. His mother came over once, drunk, and demanded to take my months-old son to the country. When I refused, she became furious, insinuating that the baby might not be his. Her words cut deep, adding to the weight of my already overwhelming situation, she was controlling.

WHEN YOU'RE COVERED BY THE BLOOD OF JESUS AND DON'T EVEN KNOW IT

The pressure of it all began to break me down again. I returned to alcohol and drugs to cope, finding solace in their numbing effects. What started as casual drink here and there quickly spiraled into a habit all over again, finding ways to escape my reality. My mother stepped in to help care for my son, giving me the opportunity to find a brief escape from the reality. During this time, I chose to numb my pain with alcohol and drugs. I buried the inner me so deep beneath the intoxication that I started to lose sight of who I was.

By the time my son turned one, I had convinced myself that I was free. Temporarily escape from the responsibilities, temporarily escape from the pain, and temporarily escape from the judgment of others. But that freedom was an illusion. People around me kept reminding me that I had a child, but I was too consumed by anger and hurt to care. I loved my son, but I felt trapped and overwhelmed. I couldn't explain my pain, so I numbed it instead.

I became known for all the wrong reasons. People called me names—trifling, bitch, and worse. Over time, I started to believe the things they said about me. I felt worthless, and all I wanted was to escape from my family, from my life, from everything. I started going out more, hitting clubs and parties, trying to find something—anything—that would make me feel better.

I got a part-time job and tried to show some responsibility, but it didn't last. I was receiving help from the state—$340 checks, food stamps, and WIC for my son. But the job lasted only six months. I started hanging out with a coworker, and that became my new escape. We would stop at a carryout after work, drinking in the parking lot until the early hours of the morning. It felt good to be away from everything, to pretend that I was temporarily escape from my reality.

But reality has a way of catching up. One morning, my son wasn't feeling well. I took him to the doctor, who diagnosed him with an ear infection and a cold. I got his medicine and started giving it to him, but the guilt of neglecting him was gnawing at me. Despite everything, I couldn't stop. I continued to spiral deeper into my destructive habits.

The day came when my son became seriously ill again. I rushed him to the hospital, where they told me he had a severe spinal infection, likely caused by a virus. He was admitted for ten days. I tried to be there for him, sitting by his side, but as soon as I left the hospital, I turned to alcohol to cope. The guilt and fear were too much to bear, and I couldn't face the reality of what was happening. I felt like a complete failure.

As my son began to recover, I realized I couldn't continue living the way I was. I had to stay home and take care of him. It scared me to my core, but I knew it was the right thing to do. I focused on him, trying to make up for the time I had lost. But the weight of my mistakes lingered, and the shame was unbearable.

One day, while walking home from picking up my son's prescription, a man called out to me in the park. We talked for a few minutes, exchanged numbers, and started seeing each other. It felt like things were going from bad to worse. He introduced me to more drinking, and soon enough, it became our way of bonding. We spent hours together, drinking until I couldn't walk. I felt like this time was different, like maybe he was someone who understood me. But in reality, I was just repeating the same patterns, falling deeper into a cycle of self-destruction.

We decided to move in together, scraping together enough money to rent an apartment. But it didn't take long for things to start falling apart. We both worked odd jobs, barely making ends meet. The money we earned was spent recklessly, and we struggled to keep up with the rent. My son was constantly sick, and I felt like I couldn't catch a break. We moved from one apartment to another, always chasing the illusion of stability but never finding it.

Then, I found out I was pregnant again. My oldest son was just a year old. I thought things might be different this time, but deep down, I knew they wouldn't be. The cycle continued— struggling to make ends meet, dealing with the emotional and physical toll of another pregnancy, and feeling more lost than ever.

His family suddenly wanted to see my oldest son after being absent for so long. I was shocked, but I let them take him a few times. After that, they disappeared again, leaving me to pick up the pieces. I was trying so hard to hold it all together, but I was more lost than ever. That dark place inside me grew stronger, whispering that I should just give up.

Before I knew it, I had baby number two. It was all happening so fast. My early twenties were a blur of pregnancies, responsibilities, and trying to keep my head above water. Everyone around me started to see him for what he really was—someone who wasn't good for me. But I loved him, even as I lost everything in the process.

We broke up and got back together more times than I can count. He saw our son only a handful of times. Eventually, I had to move back in with my mom, bringing my three children with me. I was so embarrassed and ashamed. I cried a lot, feeling like I had failed, like I was stuck with babies while everyone else moved on with their lives.

Living with my mom was like being in a detention center. The rules were strict, and I had to make sure my kids were my responsibility. I was still getting a monthly check, food stamps, and WIC, but the money would be gone within days. Staying there was suffocating, and all I could think about was how to get back on my own. I spent two years trying to figure it out, asking around, and looking for any opportunity.

Finally, I found someone willing to split the rent with me. It eased my mind for a while, and I felt like I was getting somewhere. Getting the kids into a new school was a challenge, but at least I was trying. For a brief moment, it felt like things might actually get better.

Chapter 3: Deeper And Deeper

That's when things really started to change. They say you never truly know someone until you live with them, and those words couldn't have been more true for me. I was just so happy to finally be free—free from the confines of my past, free to live on my own terms—that I didn't give much thought to anything else. We both discussed how we would navigate this new chapter in our lives, laying down the rules—the dos and don'ts—that would govern our household. We agreed on the importance of maintaining a space just for us, a sanctuary that would remain undisturbed by outsiders. But things quickly spiraled out of control.

When you're caught up in the excitement of newfound freedom, it's easy to overlook the subtle changes that start creeping into your life. People began to visit, and before I knew it, these occasional visitors turned into overnight guests. Again and again, they came, disrupting the peace and harmony we had promised each other. The situation became unbearable, and I found myself growing more and more resentful. Our home, which was supposed to be a refuge, had become a revolving door for others, and I began to catch an attitude about it. We had made a promise to each other that no one would disrupt our household, but that promise was quickly broken, leaving me feeling betrayed and disillusioned.

One day, while taking a walk to the liquor store, we ran into a friend of hers. They talked, catching up on old times, and then we all talked together. I ended up exchanging numbers with her friend, but it wasn't out of any real interest—it was more out of a sense of necessity. I wanted someone to talk to as well, someone who could fill the void that was beginning to grow inside me. Soon enough, this new friend started coming over after work, and it became a regular thing. We'd feed the kids, put them to bed, and then retreat into our own world—drinking, smoking weed, and losing ourselves in the haze of it all. What began as occasional get-togethers quickly turned into an everyday ritual. We were living recklessly, with no regard for the consequences, and before I knew it, we were both pregnant.

At this point in my life, I had completely lost touch with myself. I didn't love myself anymore, didn't care about anything or anyone. When I had my son, I was alone once again—without the father, without any real support system to lean on. My life became a downward spiral of self-destruction, fueled by alcohol and drug abuse. From the moment I woke up to the moment I passed out, I stayed lit. I couldn't face the reality of my mistakes sober, so I didn't. Instead, I spent my life trying to escape from the chaos I had created. I always felt like my kids would be better off with someone else, someone who could give them the love and stability they deserved. I didn't feel like I deserved them, and I surely didn't like myself.

Eventually, the weight of it all became too much to bear, and I decided to move again, hoping to leave behind the wreckage of my past. I reconnected with someone, and after about a year, we decided to get married. I thought that maybe, just maybe, this would finally give me the family I had always longed for. But deep down, I knew that the inner darkness still lingered, lurking just beneath the surface. I couldn't be completely honest with anyone, not even myself. I kept thinking that having kids, dating men, and getting married would somehow change the way I felt, that it would fill the emptiness inside me. But I was miserable, and I knew that nobody would understand the turmoil I was going through. So I kept it all inside, bound by my own darkness, suffocating under the weight of my own secrets.

During my 11-year marriage, I believed I had finally found something better than any relationship I had experienced before. But that illusion shattered when the darkness crept back in, consuming me all over again. I started to feel emotionally unstable, like I was teetering on the edge of a breakdown. The neglect I had for my kids was unbearable, but I didn't know how to be their mom or how to treat myself as a person. I was a people pleaser, always bending over backward to make others happy, but it was never enough. I was called all kinds of names, accused of being selfish and ungrateful, but I couldn't help it— I was lost. When I finally decided to live my truth and embrace my identity as a gay woman, it felt like a huge weight had been lifted off my shoulders. For the first time, I felt free, like I could finally breathe. But living as a gay woman was completely different from anything I had ever experienced before.

Women are delicate creatures, requiring a level of attention and care that I wasn't used to giving. I had to learn so much about myself and my new identity in the process. My kids were older by then, and I thought I was finally finding myself, finally living my truth. But I was still struggling with that inner darkness, that feeling of being pressured and unsure if I was doing anything right. Adjusting to my new life was the most difficult role I had ever taken on. I always felt like I was in a dark place, wondering why I was even here. Drinking became my way of trying to explain my feelings, but no one was really listening. People were just there for whatever I had to offer, and I didn't realize that they weren't genuine. I just wanted someone to love me, someone to fill the void inside me, but instead, I started losing myself even more.

My first relationship with a woman ended badly, I was left in pieces. The relationship had lasted five years, but it ended in disaster. I was stalked, stabbed, and taken back and forth to court. When it was finally over, I was left paranoid, constantly looking over my shoulder, afraid that the nightmare would start all over again. I had to get another place, but I knew I couldn't afford it. I worked part-time, scraping by just to have a roof over my head. My life was in shambles, and I didn't know if I was coming or going. I had never stayed anywhere for more than six months to a year, and in the midst of my madness, I turned to dating apps, hoping to find some semblance of connection, some relief from the loneliness that was consuming me.

There was one more woman who I had known and dealt with for eight years on and off. She had a strong hold on me, and no matter how much time passed, we always picked up right where we left off. But it wasn't just her—I had two or three other women in my life at all times. I felt like I had to catch up on all the times I had missed out on, but my life was full of lies and deceit. I thought I was enjoying myself, living my truth, but deep down, I was still lost, still searching for something that I couldn't quite find.

Women after women came into my life, some who genuinely cared for me and others who couldn't let go. For some reason, I always felt that when I got close to someone, I never wanted them to leave. I couldn't figure out why, but I started to do anything to keep them around. That was a lot of my problem— I needed attention, and I was impatient to see if I could make them fall in love with me. But once they did, I lost interest. Some women cried, got totally upset, and asked what was wrong with me, but I couldn't give them an answer. The selfish part of me kept promising them time, and many held on because they had fallen in love with me. They always said there was something about me, something that drew them in, but I was so clingy, jealous, and afraid of losing something that loved me.

I was trapped so far in darkness that I didn't see any other way out. I went from job to job, just trying to survive, but it was never enough. My life was reckless, self-destructive, and my kids were trapped in my madness, suffering because of my inability to get my life together. I was always angry, and the saying "hurt people hurt people" became my reality. I didn't see any way out of the cycle I was in, even as I went through seven different relationships. After my marriage ended, I had to survive, taking any job that came my way, no matter how menial or low-paying.

But the last two jobs were different. I finally got tired of going from job to job, scraping by with no real direction or purpose. I started looking for something permanent, something with benefits that could offer me some stability. Before that, I had been working as a clerk in a supermarket, I was exhausted in going to work, traveling from DC to VA for $7.25 an hour, four days a week, just to barely make $500 a week. Management in the supermarket treated me horribly, but I knew I needed more. My feet and body were always hurting, and I barely got any sleep. I was renting a room for $100 a week, going back and forth, and I kept thinking that there had to be more to life than this.

But even as I searched for something better, I couldn't shake the feeling that I was trapped in a cycle of darkness and despair. I didn't know what else to do, didn't know how to break free from the chains that bound me. All I knew was that I needed to survive, to keep pushing forward, even if it felt like I was going nowhere. My life was a constant struggle, a battle against the inner demons that threatened to consume me, and I didn't know how much longer I could hold on.

Chapter 4: The Power of Transformation

There was this woman at the bus stop; I used to see her after work, always around the same time after my shift at the supermarket. For four days straight, we used to catch the same bus at the same time. We had small talk and finally exchanged numbers. From then on, we started talking about traveling, people, and life in general. Over time, we developed an understanding and peeled back the layers of each other's personalities bit by bit.

As I served my notice period at the supermarket, a growing sense of excitement was filling in me, happiness and anticipation were transparent. I had a new job lined up, one that paid more than I had ever imagined. Everything seemed to be falling into place and I was looking forward to the three-day orientation coming up. And better yet, it turned out that the same woman was employed there as well. She always brimmed with cheerful energy and enthusiasm, and she used to go above and beyond—whether she would stay late or stepping up when no one else would. It seemed like I had struck gold; not only did I have a job with good pay, but I also had a life in every aspect.

Everything seemed to be going on track, and when one of my friends invited me to church, I immediately accepted it. I was grateful to God for he had blessed me with such a tremendous opportunity and a positive friend. Despite attending church on a regular basis, a sense of discontent remained there.

Wrestling with my urges and desires, I was struggling with myself, battling with the attraction and enticement towards women. My last relationship of eight years ended up leaving me with unresolved emotions and a never-ending war. Whenever I saw her, my heart skipped a beat with a quick pulse. I confided in her with my deepest, darkest secrets that I would not dare to share with anyone else. She was a secret I hid from the world, a secret that had to be kept hidden, despite the unclear reason behind it.

A month passed by my struggles remained the same as I battled my faith and desires side by side. However, it grew even stronger when two more women made their way into my life as if they were in line for their turns. Although I did not intend to hurt anyone, I could not stop myself from forming a bond with them. A part of me was aware of the consequences and wanted to refrain from growing too close, but the other part of me couldn't resist the connection. Later, I took a detour from my faith and dated one of the women, but the relationship ended. The other two women didn't fill the void either. I brought them along to the church, thinking that I would direct them toward the right path, guided by God, but it didn't work out very well.

Over time, spending more time in church brought a positive change in me and paved the way to strengthen my faith. My battle against myself had me worn out; I was having trouble reconciling both versions of myself, the one I was becoming and the one I had been. I was rigid with my desire for women, and my church visits did not seem to help overcome it, not at the time at least. I was well aware that something needed to change, but I wasn't certain how to go about it and what exactly would make it happen.

Soon after my first work anniversary, my life witnessed a pivotal moment. I got baptized, and most of my conversations seemed to revolve around Jesus and religion. My friend who invited me to church observed these changes in me. She was someone I used to share my struggles with, but as I grew closer to God, I unknowingly began to distance myself from her.

As the tug-of-war became intense, my life started becoming even messier. First, I lost my apartment, which I barely managed to keep for a year and a half. Despite knowing that it wasn't under my budget, I went ahead and applied for the place due to the urgency of having a roof over my head. I had to juggle between my work and three different relationships. And finally, it was gone.

Every day felt like being on the edge of the unknown, swaying between stability and chaos; not just in my personal life, my work was falling apart as well. With the new management that did not care about us and was mostly short-staffed, I was restless and in discomfort, due to the pain and sore muscles. My legs, back, feet, ankles, and not a single body part were in good shape, and the off days were not enough to recover from that state. I pushed myself to a great extent and took a break when I was in dire need. I did not lose hope and continued to pray, but nothing seemed to be on track. I wished for a better life, to be freed from the relentless work and abusive jobs that treated their employees like a bunch of nobodies. I shared my grievances with my pastor, including the relationships that were weighing on me.

My work life was on the brink when they brought up unbearable demands. We had to either give in to their impossible demands, or hand in our resignations, they were very well aware of the fact that we needed this job, and they took advantage of our vulnerability. Having no other source of income, I had to keep on with the workplace abuse, which only got worse. From then on, my life felt consumed by darkness, and all I longed for was to break free from a slave-like life. I would retreat to the restroom at work, crying and praying; it had become my war room.

Despite all these hardships, I did not stop going to church. I began to understand the high turnover at work. I had become a hollow soul, screaming inside for help. Although I had women in my life, they weren't enough to help me out spiritually. I had their physical support, which was also something I yearned for. It felt like I did not want those women in my life, but at the same time, I could not bear the thought of being alone. I found myself bouncing from one relationship to another but ended up hurting myself in this course of action. A part of me was pushing me to keep going while the other had convinced me that nothing would change.

Finally, the day came; I burst out and finally cried out for help.

Out of the blue, we were called in for a meeting at work, and it turned out that our current boss was fired, leaving us wondering about our fate. Are they going to keep us? Are they going to lay us off? No one knew. A week later, new management took over, changing everything—new schedules, new rules—and only four other people remained from the original team. We were all walking on eggshells.

As I came back home one day, I pondered about my life and the decisions I had made so far. I discussed this with my pastor, who prophesied about what was coming next at my workplace, which did not seem like useful information, and it certainly did not make going to work any easier. If anything, my mind was all over the place. As if these problems weren't enough, my relationships with the women were getting even more intense. It dawned on me that I had a fear of rejection. Although I had control over each one of those women, I was still going through so much emotionally.

One morning at work, one of my colleagues called in sick, and I had to perform her tasks as well. It was incredibly hard, and they had zero remorse for my situation. All they did was watch me tackle the workload with no regard for the pain; I was crying a river inside. It was unbearable and went on for two weeks. Eventually, it came to my attention that the guy who assisted me was no longer working there. At times, they brought in temporary help, but nothing permanent.

My shift used to end late in the evening, and I rode with a coworker. One of my friends, after having this knowledge, offered me a ride back home as her workplace was 15 minutes away from mine. It was sweet of her to offer. Every night, on our way back, we would strike up a conversation. My physical pain was evident, and my groans while sitting in the car had become a norm.

At that point, I was in dire need of getting everything out of my system, or the depression would have weighed me down. Therefore, I sought therapy. I was not an open book; the only ones who knew my struggles were God, my pastor, and the women I was involved with, at that time.

My mother used to say, *"Always be thankful for having a job."* It left me feeling like I had no choice but to handle whatever came my way. I knew I needed to move again, but I was exhausted from constantly relocating, so I chose to rent a room instead. I was juggling between church, therapy, my women, a few associates, and a job that was eating me slowly.

Soon enough, the workload at the job went beyond my limitations, and I found myself in a constant hysteria. It hadn't been a week since I was asked to restock all the rooms and kitchen. It was certainly not a one-person job, but bit by bit, I finished it all by myself. This constant grapple had worn me down, but through all this, I felt the energy of the Lord that had been pushing me forward, making me feel special. Not that it always felt good, but my urge to change had me seek Him seriously.

As I noticed a shift in my relationship — though I couldn't explain it — I gradually lost interest and withdrew from it. I was well aware of my physical needs. I was so frustrated with life that I cried so many days and nights, just to continue to go to work.

One day when I was stocking up alone, I experienced severe back pain, which then led me to take 3 to 6 Advil per day, just to get through work. *My God will meet all your needs according to the richest of his glory in Jesus Christ,* philippians 4:19. To get some rest, I started calling in sick and availed my PTOs. Although I knew they would raise questions about this, I did not go to work. After all, I had exhausted myself to the extent that it was affecting my overall health.

After a few months, I experienced severe discomfort in my lower back, as if something had popped. I did not give it too much attention, swallowed painkillers, and went through the day. I made up my mind that I would look into it tomorrow, on my day off.

As I lay there, taking pills, feeling both weary and sore, I attempted to get up and go to the restroom, but I couldn't stand straight. Immediately, I reached out to my manager, informing them of my condition and that I was heading to the doctor's office. They provided me with my prescription and granted me a week off. I mentioned that this pain felt unlike anything I had experienced before, and despite my hopes, it didn't improve at all throughout the week.

Since my condition escalated during work, they had to approve my sick leave as I handed them my doctor's note.

By God's grace and mercy, I was still holding myself together. My pastor prayed for me and my future, my job, and my relationships. Now, I was in my vulnerable state, uncertain of my next steps. But I had my hopes up as the father above had a plan for me.

A few days later, I visited the doctor, who told me I couldn't return to work. Naturally, there's no such thing as light duty in a kitchen. At that visit, I learned that I had spinal stenosis, though the doctor at the time had not disclosed it to me initially.

With the job gone, for the first time in my life, I was free... when you know who you are, and whose you are...

The big difference is that the old things fade away to make room for the new, walking in my purpose of spreading the gospel of Jesus Christ is a beautiful position... I thank God for his Grace and mercy over me...

And his favor, anointing, also peace, joy, and the gift of love all from God, his unconditional love is amazing...

I couldn't find it in this world, the peace I have the world didn't give it to me and the world can't take it away.

As I took these first steps toward my new life, the young woman who had been with me noticed a change in me. She said, "You've changed."

Despite the physical pain and struggles with my spinal injury, I knew I was fortunate. It felt like I was living in a spiritual trance, with the Lord and angels by my side. Every day felt like a walk through a spiritual wonderland, and the more I experienced, the more I realized I had become a walking, talking testimony.

One night, I had a vivid dream where I was battling a tin man, and after a fierce fight, I finally defeated him. Another night, I found myself walking down a dark road, burdened by a heavy bag. Then, Jesus came to me, took my hand, and led me out of the darkness. Through these dreams and visions, I knew that God was speaking to me through every trial.

As I spent more time in prayer and reflection, I began to understand what my pastor had been trying to tell me. At first, I struggled with the message, but over time, my relationship with God deepened in ways I had never experienced.

Then, during a church service, the pastor addressed a topic that hit me hard: homosexuality.

This triggered a storm of emotions and confusion within me. I had been involved in relationships with women, and my mind was constantly occupied with their beauty. But the spirit of lust had taken hold of me, turning into an obsession. I didn't even realize how many different spiritual influences were at play, controlling my thoughts and actions. The weight of guilt and shame grew heavier as I began to reflect on everything that was happening inside me.

One day, a friend asked me directly about my views on homosexuality, and that question triggered a wave of anxiety and depression. My mind was consumed with the women I had been involved with. I felt trapped in a cycle, unable to escape the pull of my desires. This struggle forced me to ask myself an uncomfortable question: What was I choosing—my relationship with God or my desires?

I chose to follow the Holy Spirit's guidance, even though it cost me friendships and connections along the way. Losing my mother, on top of everything else happening at the time, was completely devastating, and I needed God more than ever.

As I began to withdraw from these relationships, I unintentionally hurt my friend, who had been a big part of my life. She cried, cursed at me, and felt betrayed. It was one of the hardest decisions I ever had to make. For the first time in my life, I was truly alone. The weight of that loneliness was overwhelming, but it was what I needed to hear God more clearly.

Everything in my life felt new and unfamiliar. I was used to going out every day, staying busy. But now, with my job gone, I had to figure out simple things like how to get groceries and how to manage with limited finances. I felt lost. But the truth is, the Father, Son, and Holy Spirit do Their best work when you're alone, and I found that to be true in my own life.

Through all of this, I came to a crucial realization: so many people are fighting their own battles, carrying their own untold stories. When you go to church, it becomes clearer who you can truly trust. I've had my own issues with trust, but I've learned that I don't need to rely on anyone but the Father, Jesus, and the Holy Spirit. They are all I need. In Their eyes, I am perfect.

I share my story in the hope that it helps break someone free from their bondage or generational curses. God is a deliverer, a healer, and a provider. He gave His only begotten Son to die for my sins—and for yours. He is the key to everything in your life and can help you establish a deeper relationship with Him. I give Him all the glory.

When people ask me what I do now, I tell them I am a full-time worker for the Gospel. I've also been blessed with the gift of cooking. I'm a professional chef, and cooking brings me both comfort and joy. It's something I do to bless others, and it has become part of my purpose.

Through it all, I've learned a valuable lesson: every mess has a message, and every test has a testimony. Only God can do what you cannot. Let His will guide your life. Walk by faith, not by sight.

Chapter 5: The Savior

Let Me Tell You About Jesus

"Taste and see that the Lord is good,"

- Psalm 34:8.

As time passed, I began to distance myself from the friend who first brought me to church. We used to do everything together, but God wanted me to draw closer to Him, and He often does His best work when we're alone. I started to feel a tug-of-war within me, the Holy Spirit working on my heart, though I didn't recognize it at first. Isolation was tough, but it was necessary for my transformation.

I remember one day I was cleaning my room, where I kept all my beverages and a single bottle of platinum liquor. That bottle had been sitting there for about a month, untouched. I kept it for whoever might come by, but suddenly, I heard a voice in my spirit: "If you don't want it, don't give that poison to anyone else." That moment hit me hard. I took the bottle to the bathroom and poured it down the toilet. In that act, I knew I was different—I was changing.

The feeling that came over me was unmatched, a deep love like I had never known before. But part of me still clung to my old life. I wanted to keep both worlds, but I didn't know how to let go of the past. Frustration set in as I struggled with what to do next. I began talking regularly to God and my pastor, seeking guidance as I wrestled with the weight of it all.

When you begin to develop a relationship with God, it's like nothing else. If you try to go against His will, it feels strange, you being convicted by the Holy Spirit. I started withdrawing from people because I no longer felt right doing the same things as before. I even pretended with my friends for a while, not wanting to lose them all at once, but it didn't last. Everyone around me noticed the change.

The Holy Spirit has a way of making you think deeply, giving you wisdom and clarity for what's next in your journey. He lets you know about people, places, and things that no longer align with your path. Even when life gets hard and tests your faith, God speaks to us if we're willing to listen. It's a journey filled with lessons and blessings, one that repeats until we reach the destination He has for us.

He knew me before I knew myself. He knew this day would come, and He knew this story would be told. He knew I would be set free. And He knows you, too. He created you, and He wants to set you free just as He did for me. If you're reading this, know that He's waiting for you to surrender and come to Him. The Bible is real, and for every situation in your life, there's a verse

"He will never leave you nor forsake you."

Hebrews 13:5

"He will supply all your needs."

- Philippians 4 :19

Satan wants to keep you trapped, but God offers a second chance. Every day, I try to live in a way that pleases Him, even when obstacles arise, because He always shows up and shows out—that's my Heavenly Father.

The Years 2020–2022

Between 2020 and 2022, I faced unimaginable loss. First, my mom passed away, and nine months later, my uncle died. Then, on April 19, 2021, my nine-year-old grandson passed away. Nineteen months of death and loss, something I had never experienced before. In the past, I would have turned to my friends, gone to the liquor store, and drowned my sorrows in alcohol. But this time, God gave me peace and strength.

Even in the midst of such profound loss, I continued to spread the gospel of Jesus Christ. We all have our own bag of sins to deal with every day, but there is power in the blood of Jesus. As John 15:4–9 says, "Dwell in me, and I will dwell in you. Just as no branch can bear fruit by itself without abiding in the vine, neither can you bear fruit unless you abide in me."

God is God, and this is His story. He gets all the glory. I am just His vessel.

Poverty-spiritual meaning

A state of humility and dependence on God is considered a virtue and a path to blessings.

The world's definition of poverty is a lack of resources—the condition of someone who does not possess a socially acceptable amount of money or material possessions.

When I was lost in sin and darkness, that was exactly my state. But now, I am free and rich in the Lord.

Amen.

Transitional housing

I was on an assignment from God during 2024–2025, for 1 year and 5 months.

Every day at this facility, I didn't know what to expect—but God did. He wanted to use me, and He did.

So many of the women there were broken, and I became His voice. They saw His light through me.

I spent my days encouraging, praying, and listening to their stories. Day after day, they came to me for prayer, and I was learning from them, too. It was both a lesson and a blessing from God.

I also had the joy of cooking for many, and it filled me with so much happiness.

Now, I visit at least twice a month, and they always welcome me with open arms. I just love seeing them again.

Thank You, Father, for using me.

Reflection on Life

Even before I truly knew Him, I encountered so many people and always felt that God was present, even when I was still a sinner. As I began to build my relationship with Him, I tried to bring others along, praying for their souls and salvation.

What I've realized is that some people carry bigger burdens than others, but we all have our own bags of sins, and Jesus Christ died for them all.

God bless you all, and I hope my story inspires you.

Isaiah 41:10 so do not fear for I am with you do not be dismayed for I am your God I will strengthen you and help you I will up hold you with my righteous hand.

Personal Reflection – April 2025, Easter Holiday

This Easter, April 2025, was a divine moment in my life. After nearly four years apart, my youngest son Montel and I rekindled our relationship. I had missed my grandbabies so much—it was such a joy to see them again, and they were just as excited to see me.

During that visit, I learned that Montel had written his first book—completely unaware that I had been working on mine. It will be a beautiful surprise. God's divine timing is truly unmatched. Only God.

This whole season of my life reminds me of the freedom I've found in Him. As John 8:36 says, "If the Son therefore shall make you free, ye shall be free indeed."

I'm walking in that freedom today.

Stay tuned... new beginnings are on the way.

For decades struggle

From darkness to light

The enemy want you

Bound, But God has other Plans

Ms. Tina <u>*"Deshay"*</u> Jackson
Love Yall
God Bless

d-product-compliance